ALSO BY CAROLYN MILLER

This Is Mine (2005)
After Cocteau (2002)
Constant Lover (2001)

LIGHT, MOVING

LIGHT, MOVING

Carolyn Miller

SIXTEEN RIVERS PRESS

Copyright © 2009 by Carolyn Miller
All rights reserved
Printed in Canada

My thanks to the following publications,
in which some of the poems in this book first appeared:

*Appalachia, Atlanta Review, Barnabe Review, Connecticut Review,
Constant Lover* (Protean Press), *The Gettysburg Review,
New Letters, Nimrod, Nobody's Child* (Baywood Publishing),
*Northwest Poets and Artists Calendar, Runes,
The Seattle Review, The Sewanee Review, Southern Poetry Review,
The Southern Review, This Is Mine* (Protean Press),
Urban Nature (Milkweed Editions), *Wind Bell*

Published by Sixteen Rivers Press
P.O. Box 640663
San Francisco, CA 94164
www.sixteenrivers.org

Library of Congress Control Number: 2008907853
ISBN 978-0-9767642-9-8

Cover art: *Fog Bank, San Francisco* by Carolyn Miller

Epigraph: From *The Spring of My Life*, translated by Sam Hamill; © 1997.
Reprinted by arrangement with Shambhala Publications, Inc.,
Boston, MA. www.shambhala.com.

For Frank

Just being alive!
—miraculous to be in
cherry blossom shadows!

—Issa Kobayashi, *The Spring of My Life*

Contents

The Slanted Streets
First Things   3
Matter   4
Eucharist   5
In Summer   6
Note to the Near World   7
Birthday Poem   8
Considering Flynn   10
Journal Entry   12
Celibacy   13
Fresh Gardenias Today   15
Phone Call in August   16
After Swimming in the Public Pool   17

The Memory of Light
Bridget Kelley   21
Outside My Window   23
Childhood Rivers   24
Happiness   25
Honeysuckle   26
Easter Week   27
In the Eucalyptus Grove   28
Life Support   30
Cleaning   31
November   34
December   35
Winter, Sleep, the Absence of Desire   36

In the Garden

Garden in Late Winter   41

At the End of the Drought   42

In the Garden   43

A Warm Summer in San Francisco   45

Community Garden   47

Rose Garden, Summer Solstice   48

To Dr. Williams   49

In Praise of Dirt   51

The World as It Is

Unseen Eclipse   55

Haiku for Tassajara   56

Cachagua Valley, Mid-July   60

Autumn at Muir Beach   61

Early October   62

Vermont, October   63

Crossing Mount Tam, Thanksgiving Week   64

Finding the Petroglyphs   65

Noche de Tumulto, San Miguel de Allende   67

Landing at SFO   70

Driving with Robert   71

Night in San Francisco   73

Christmas Day   74

Tuesday, 9 A.M.   75

The World as It Is   76

How Long Should You Look at the Earth's Face?   77

Notes   79

About the Author   81

The Slanted Streets

First Things

Still dark.
Still. Dark. Far out over the black
water, the foghorns low like cattle. The cable leaps awake,
knocking, clattering in its slot. The first bird calls,
a single song twining the still air. Then
another, and another wakes and calls, until
a cloud of sound rises over the backyards.
   Now the far-off rumble of the first cable car,
laboring up the hill like a heavy cargo ship
carrying the morning. Here is my life:
the slanted streets, the growing light,
the excited birds.

Matter

No matter how early I get up, the world
is already whirling; no matter
how silent the kitchen, the stove is warm,
like a great heart, the coffee beans
are sending out their dark signal,
the cat is half-awake, his second eyelids
partly glued to the two suns
of his eyes. The oranges contain themselves
like glorious planets on the cheese tray,
the milk waits, luminous in its carton,
the round table abides, the day
grows wide. Slowly I step into
its bright stream.

Eucharist

Washing dishes, I pour
a lake of water over the thin shells
streaked with fat. Honeycombs
of bubbles and bits of food race down
the drain to join the sea.
This lake is deep; I can't tell
how far the land will take us
in this ocean wind, or where
the pale, leftover orange light is leading
as night leaps toward us,
or who is transforming, or
what is being transformed: It is all
the abundant body of the Goddess, it is
the broken, risen body of Christ,
it is the mind of Buddha fixed
on the emptiness between
particles of being, his right hand
reaching down to touch the earth,
as I stand washing dishes.

In Summer

I walked out into the morning light
on the solstice, at the height of June,
in a city where trees keep their leaves and spume
the warm scent of jasmine in the night.

The sun was out, though on this edge of land,
summer days are often thick with cloud
and fog. And suddenly the growing crowd
of my dead were close at hand.

I write their birthdays on my calendar each year
so I can keep them still
part of this flux, this wide sea, this spill
of light, this whir of wings sounding in my ear.

Note to the Near World

for Frank

Drove around the Mission and South of Market,
listening to Leonard Cohen and thinking how much
you would have loved the day, filled as it was
with the fumes of poppies, smells of Mexican food,
messages from the dead in the shape of falling leaves,
the sky incandescent, cloudless, in the month
of your death, the new baseball stadium rising up
not far from the places we used to go, distant
sound of the rusty hinge of the door to the other world,
faint smell of smoke from its torches, you very close
in the month when the dead are closest,
everything slightly larger in the pulsing autumn light,
the trendy café on a back street in a converted
factory, *citron pressé* at an outdoor table,
me hoping you are somewhere listening to Monk
when not here with me, sitting in the sun.

Birthday Poem

When I was a child in the magic world,
I was magic, too. I knew
I had been singled out from others;
that was why I was alone, and why
everywhere I looked I saw a sign:
under the ground, limestone pale
as honey, honeycombed with caves;
on the earth, bobwhites and springs,
mayapples drawn up in ranks beneath the oaks;
my room floating in the branches
above the house; the Christmas trees
burning from within; the snow
folded over everything like a wing.

Now I am grown, and the bones
of my old dog are moldering
somewhere in Missouri, going to loam
under the hickory trees. But still
the world reveals to me each day that I
am blessed. As when the Muni bus
pulls up to the curb beside the crowd
to stop before me like a marriage coach.
Or when the mail slithers through the slot
with messages for me. Eggs thicken
in their shell, the yolk still molten;
in my garden the smallest seeds

turn into cabbages and carrots.
The sidewalks gleam with particles
of glitter; along the streets,
stands are filled with rows of fruit
waiting, like hostages, for me to set them free;
wooden houses, like pale steamboats, prepare
to loose themselves and sail onto the bay.
When I buy flowers, they give up their lives
for me; first their petals fade and curl,
then fall with a small sound
on the tabletop. I lie in my room as though
cupped inside a hand. The floors and walls
were cut from trees; the pillows
on my bed are filled with the down of ducks
and geese; at night I am protected by
the dark's feathered breast.
And each November, a year dies around me,
the sun slides down the sky,
and, on the coast, fog takes the shape
of a great white dragon
waiting for the rain.

Considering Flynn

after Christopher Smart

For he is the color of a fog bank over the ocean in late afternoon.
For his eyes are lined with charcoal gray like Cleopatra's.
For his nose is the same color.
For his fur is as fine as smoke, and he seems to wear a suit of velvet.
For his forehead is lined with stripes made from the fur growing in ridges, and his nose is marked with an X in the same fashion.
For he is the messenger of the living Goddess and She hums within him.
For at night he sleeps at the foot of my bed and forbears to wake me.
For he waits till I stir in the morning before he comes to sit on my chest like a sphinx.
For he patiently sits until I place the food in his bowl, and carefully cleans his whiskers after eating.
For he travels outside while I eat my breakfast, then comes back in when the teakettle whistles.
For he sits at my feet to be picked up when I drink my tea.
For he needs to be stroked and cosseted several times a day.
For he sleeps for hours on the bed or the chaise longue, giving himself over fully to the world of darkness.
For he can leap from that realm in an instant at any loud noise.
For he fears the doorbell and the vacuum cleaner.
For he goes down into the smelly, garbagey, ratty, wormy place of the trash bins and backyards and always comes home.
For he moves through the house by day, following the path of the sun.

For he has learned to make himself a warm cave under the
   comforter.
For his legs are long and he has six toes on each of his front feet.
For at rest he stretches out one long leg, languorous as an odalisque.
For he lies on his back, his legs splayed and his belly and throat
   exposed in ecstasy.
For the pupils of his yellow eyes wax and wane like the moon, and
   the inner cover of his eyes rolls back slowly when he half-awakes.
For he has never killed any living creature except the rare slow fly.
For he can leap straight up three feet in the air to catch the fly.
For he rears up on his hind feet, butting his head like a little horse
   when I hold out my hand.
For he anoints the doorjambs with his scent glands.
For he sometimes gulps with happiness when I hold him.
For his cry is small, and he purls, which is meowing with the mouth
   closed.
For his ancestor Jeoffry was beloved by a poet who went mad.
For his only faults are trying to spill his water and leaping up with
   no warning.
And upending the wastebasket in the night to chew on pieces of
   plastic.
For he is filled with Buddha nature.
For he does both the Up- and Downward-Facing Dog and, of
   course, the Cat.
For he attends to all his needs.
For he purrs.

Journal Entry

Mid-July

Walking back from the community garden along Bay Street, I reached up to pick a cluster of red flowers from a gum tree. Just as I broke it off, my hand was suddenly filled with clear liquid pouring from the open mouths of the hollow, fringed flowers. I stood stock still, shocked by the sexuality of what had just happened. After a minute or two, I put the flowers in my pocket and walked on, the liquid on my hand drying into dark, sticky streams.

Celibacy

The early-flowering plum trees have lost
most of their blossoms; a few ragged ones hang on,
overwhelmed by new leaves.
I'm always surprised by this stage of spring, when
the young, bright leaves overtake the blossoms with
a kind of violence, with nature's obsession to endure,
loving, as it does, the idea of the individual,
but not the individual.
    After a long dry spell
it rains for days, and the streams cannot contain
themselves. It must be like being touched and entered
after a long time of not being touched and entered,
like feeling semen leaking from your body;
it must be like love spilling over, love and need.
    The smell of potted hyacinths fills my flat:
that mix of rot and sexuality and longing.
Their meaty little trumpets announce
the change of seasons. My body changes
and grows old. Sex seems like another country,
one I have lost the way to, although sometimes
when I see the faces of certain men, I have the quick
sense of a door that could be opened
into new rooms. What does it mean to have a self,
the sense of self? these collections
of accommodations to the world, our baggage of wants
and compromises and unforgiving dreams? I try

to let my borders go, to let go of my self and feel
the endless, rocking ocean in which we swim,
but I am caught in a small pool of afternoon
and rotting hyacinths.

    On television I see the surface of Venus,
brought into my room across millions of black miles.
It is flexible and burning, glowing red-orange waves
striated with light, undulating, pulsing
like the walls of the birth canal,
an ocean all of fire. In that molten place there are no selves
to look back at us, divided here: blue and green,
land and water, drought and flood, joined
and alone.

Fresh Gardenias Today

Breathing thickly under cellophane, fitted carefully into
cardboard boxes, they lie in the cool, stopped time
of the florist's, drugged by their own perfume,
small spheres of liquid resting on their heavy lunar petals,
damp and smooth as curls of ivory butter.

Though I touched just the stem, careful not to bruise
the creamy skin, when I pinned the heavy flower to my dress
I was drawn at once into its slow, voluptuous death,
my every step enclouded with the lush smell of mortality.
    The next day, I woke up in his bed, my dress
lying wrinkled on the floor, the gardenia crushed, creased,
veined with rust, but still pouring out
its worldly odor, mingling its insistent fragrance with
his sweet-sour animal smell.

Phone Call in August

for Tom

Someone called me. It was when we lived in the big flat on North Point Street. The phone was in the hall, in a kind of alcove. The walls were white, and there was a window behind the table where the phone was. I don't remember who called me, but that person told me you were dead. I thought, *How can that be possible?* It had never occurred to me that you could die, then or ever. It was nighttime. It must have been around nine o'clock, because I remember that my children were in their room. I was talking on the phone to the person who had called me when I started crying. After I hung up, I kept on crying, but it was not the kind of crying I had ever done, not even when my marriage ended. I was making a sound I had never made before, a sound I didn't know that I could make. I went into my small bedroom. The walls were the color of a certain kind of rose, the mauvey blue that some red roses turn when they start to die. I don't know how long I lay on my bed, crying in that way, but I remember thinking that my daughters were angry with me for crying, because they didn't come to comfort me or even to ask what was wrong. But now I think they must have been so frightened.

After Swimming in the Public Pool

Riding the bus home at twilight: The sky retains blue light like a sponge, and the lights of the city glow in the half-day, half-night like strings of Christmas lights, or lights seen from underwater, and I can't help thinking that all this has been created just to please me. Up the hill step wooden buildings ornamented with moldings and brackets, topped with cornices and swagged with garlands, each one as elaborate as a birthday cake.

Sunlight comes through the glass wall of North Beach Pool in the afternoon, and the clear aqua water is ribboned through with sun. When I took a shower after swimming today, a woman with dark hair to her waist stood next to me. Her tan line was high up on her buttocks, and she had large, full breasts with spreading nipples the color of red raspberries.

At home, I lie down on my bed, dazzled by the world. Early evening, swimming in my own happiness, my muscles tired, my hair still damp, the faint odor of chlorine rising from my skin.

The Memory of Light

Bridget Kelley

> *Peter and Bridget Kelley immigrated*
> *to Saint Louis, Missouri . . . around 1844.*
> *. . . [their] daughter Julia Ann married*
> *Richard Miller in 1862.*
>
> —From *Our Family Record:*
> *Miller-Kelley-Page-Vaughan*

We worked the potato fields, in the deep,
spongy soil as black as the hearts
of the English, who owned the land.
Every day we ate hard bread and drank
bitter water for breakfast, then
wrapped ourselves to dig in the mist
that rose up from the fields. I remember the wet
dirt seemed to stretch for miles, curving
over the low hills of County Cork
and on to the sea, and I remember the smell of it,
thick and rich, like a home that we had come from.
When the leaves of the potato plants turned pale green,
then yellow, and the days began to grow short again
and draw us down toward winter, we dug into the dirt
with our hands, feeling for the bright, hard potatoes
like prizes in the dark, and we filled
the sacks that we dragged behind us until
we could no longer move them. Then a year came
when we pulled up potatoes dark with the blight,
rotten and stinking to heaven,
as if death were under the ground, eating

the only food that could keep us alive.
We cut out the blasted eyes and tried to plant them,
and bred shrunken things riddled with disease.
It seemed as if God had turned his back on us
and had closed his ears to our praying, and
the English left us without any pay
and locked up their great houses. So Peter and I,
still young, and with only the two little girls,
dug the jar out from the packed dirt floor,
and we took every farthing, and Grandmother Maeve's
embroidered tablecloth. We left the dog
to make his own way, and we took the blue bowl
and the turnip watch that had belonged
to Great-Uncle Liam, and I wrapped Julia and Kathryn
in the only good quilts we had, and we walked
two days and a night till we came to the sea,
where the fever ship, not much larger than our sod house,
rocked like a toy on the world's green edge.

Outside My Window

In summer, a cloud of leaves hovered over
the branches, a rich depth of leaf and sun
greening the light of the room. Then the color
faded, waned, and the light grew gold and red
as the trees burst silently into flame.
Gradually all color dropped away, and the light
grew pale. Sometimes it flashed off snow
and ice on brilliant branches, or spilled like milk
through the bare black twigs. In spring,
a wash of color was reflected from the new
green and white oak leaves, emerging like small hands
that would draw me into their grasp,
that would hold my life in their keeping
and never let it go.

Childhood Rivers

You must approach them slowly, for they are
rimmed with green fur and slippery stones. The smell
of them rises up and you walk through it,
like velvet curtains parting. The pebbles clank
beneath your feet, and dragonflies sail by, purple-
blue and iridescent, and the fur stirs in the green
water, and tadpoles waggle through, and leeches
and sucker fish try to grab your toes, and the air
above the water opens like a promise that will be fulfilled
over and over in your life, this mix of danger and solace,
fear and sudden joy, as if you could become part of the river
and at the same time rise above it on your dragon-dark,
rainbow-silvered wings.

Happiness

For many years of my life I was foolish, wasting
my time, loving the wrong people,
not loving the others enough. I wanted so much,
so many things—there was no end to my wanting,
to the hunger that filled me up. For most of my life
I was happy only for moments,
like the time in high school we drove to the lake
in someone's old rattly car, and on the way back
stopped to rent horses and rode them
in the rain. So long ago, I don't remember
who I was with or where we were, but
I remember my wet hair, my wet clothes,
and the wide, smooth haunches of the horses,
as round and taut as apples, shining
with water, stinking of horse, brushing against
the coarse, tangled undergrowth,
releasing the smell of leaves and green
on the muddy path.

Honeysuckle

How it bloomed every spring in the scraggly woods,
holding out long golden tongues and stamens
under its curled upper petals. How its dragon heads nodded
among the ovate green leaves.
How it sent out a cloud that smelled just like honey
alongside the reeking white flower globes of the wild onions.
How I tore off its blossoms and sucked out the nectar.
How it came back every year without fail, though everything
changed around it. How it told me that in the midst
of bitterness there would be pockets of sweetness. How it still
says to me, year after year, *come back, come back, come back.*

Easter Week

It was all still there: from the plane, the rusted
tin barn roofs, the twisting rivers, the pale mauve
and gray-green woods. On the rental car radio,
tornado warnings; a thunderstorm
was blowing in from the west as I drove on the interstate,
past green fields and old limestone outcroppings.
Jonquils and daffodils were blooming in my mother's
ruined yard, and the lilac bush was in flower.
On the way to the hospital, the storm hit;
rain blackened the tree trunks in the bare woods,
dogwood blooming in drifts on the hills.
My mother, her eyes turned the clouded blue-gray of an infant,
tried to speak but could not. When she fell asleep,
I sat and watched her trying to live,
the pulse beating in her throat, the vein on her forehead
branching out like lightning.

In the Eucalyptus Grove

Like my mother, the towering trees have lost their hold
on the earth. After the great winter storm, the park
is devastated, the huge, peeling eucalyptuses
lying at angles, crushing the younger trees,
the cypresses dangling useless branches like
my mother's right leg and arm. When I spoke
to her on the phone, she was frightened and weeping.
She said, "Oh, Carolyn! My nerves is gone!" I knew then
how bad it was—my mother, so proud
of her good grammar, learned at teachers' college
her first time away from home.

Finally, two days without rain; the bikers and skaters
are out. Storm debris—old pinecones, twigs, twisted streamers
of eucalyptus bark—litters the green winter grass.
Each year she had grown weaker, more unsteady on her feet.
Once she fell on the hillside and had to crawl
all the way back to the house. After the final fall, she cried out,
"What's happening to me?" No one knew for sure, but we knew
that her roots had pulled up out of the red clay, past
the raw yellow stones inside the hill.

"I'm going to start learning to walk again,"
she said after a few weeks, her words slurred, her body
heavy and stiff in the nursing home bed. "I'm going to start
tomorrow." But the physical therapist told us,

"She's old and tired. And it's been too long. If you wait too long,
the body forgets how to balance itself." It was the first time
I understood the intricate dance of body and earth.
But it was months before we understood
she would never walk again, that a storm in her brain
had made her fall like a great tree surrendering
to earth's pull. The earth that never gives up
wanting us back, wanting to fold us into it like
a mother holds her child.

Life Support

The end was pathetic, full of pathos, that
bottomless, aching sorrow for one who suffers
and for yourself for suffering in turn.
Time stretched on and on in the nursing home,
months into years of being fed, being turned,
being changed, years of white sheets and strange faces,
sleep blurring nights and days and weeks,
her eyes surrounded by purple shadows, her skin
growing almost transparent, her body weaker and
weaker until she could not speak or even swallow.
For so long she had held on to life, a strong woman
with the habit of endurance, and when it came time
to decide whether or not to let her go, we held on;
we could not give her up, the mother we'd tried so hard
to escape; we could not let her starve, the mother
who had fed us for so many years and so well.
And so we let them feed her through a tube, the mother
we could not imagine not having, though we were haunted
by the fear that her hooded eyes were begging for deliverance.

A thousand miles away in California, I watched the hawks
that sometimes fly over the city, wishing that somehow she
could rise out of her body, that my mother,
with her fierce raptor's eyes and useless arms, could,
with just one downward thrust, be carried on a spiral of warm air
to the heaven she believed in.

Cleaning

First I moved all the papers out of the kitchen,
the greeting cards and letters and the lists
written in my mother's beautiful, shaky
hand. I moved stacks of magazines and bills
and piles of notices from the Reader's Digest
Sweepstakes off the gray Formica breakfast table,
and took cups and glasses full of ballpoint pens, bobby pins,
thumbtacks, razor blades, old keys, and coins
off the wavy linoleum counter, and old phone books
and piles of papers with names and telephone numbers
and put everything beside the boxes and baskets
of photographs and the leaning towers
of *Reader's Digest*s and Southern Baptist bulletins
and the dying begonias in the sun room. Then
I took out the vacuum cleaner
and went through the house, sweeping up
the dust that layered everything in the home
of a woman who believed that dust was sinful,
cleaning under the bed and pulling out balled-up socks,
dusting the venetian blinds and sucking up dead
leaves and cobwebs and fallen plaster, and I cleaned
the bathtub and the toilet, working as fast as I could
without stopping, sweating and breathing hard.
Then I took the towels off the recliner and the worn sofa,
I stripped the sheets off the bed and the cases
off the pillows, and I sorted through the piles of dirty clothes

and I washed the socks and pajamas and underwear,
using the blue Cheer in the plastic container. Then
I dried everything in the failing Maytag and
folded the warm clothes. Next I went through the house
moving the ugliest vases and teapots and bowls
and ceramic statues downstairs to the basement,
rearranging and grouping and adjusting, trying
to get it all back to the way it was when I was a child,
when my mother was young and strong, and finally I went outside
and picked up the shingles that had blown off the roof
and pulled up some of the weeds that had invaded
the yard and straightened the fallen flowerpots
and put the rusting lawn chair back where it was
when my mother sat and watched the birds at twilight.
And then, the last day of my stay almost over,
I walked out into the woods, where I hadn't gone
until now, though they were filled with blooming dogwood
and redbud and a soft gray-brown multiplicity of branches,
and even though the path had disappeared,
I walked through the dry layer of oak leaves
that covered the floor of the woods to my old place,
the little clearing above the limestone cave
that, long ago, at just this time of year,
I had decorated as an Easter surprise for my mother.
Now there was no nest of colored eggs,
or crepe paper streamers in the trees, no Easter bunnies

in the grass, but as though they had been waiting all this time,
small bouquets of Johnny-jump-ups
were blossoming among the dead leaves. I sat,
looking at the flooded valley far below, in the woods
where I had spent long days
climbing rocks and dreaming on the moss,
and I said to myself: *This is not my home anymore.*

November

Now I am pulled down
into the earth, out of the fields
of flowers into the wound
that opens at my feet. I hear the long
dry creak of the door that leads
to death, I see the crevice
widen, the world split
apart without warning: the white faces
of the flowers disappearing,
the day gone cold, the color drained
from everything, the dark lord
of time emerging from the ground
to take me, my mother
left alone, unmoving,
stunned, the gold sheaves fallen
from her arms.

December

I go down among the roots and shadows, corms
and carapaces, the closed, secret seeds, the broken
ends of the ruined year. It is dark here, and cold,
and the darkness deepens; the wet walls shine black
in the wavering torchlight; the air is furred
with the smell of mold. So many souls are lost here;
I call to them, but they cannot answer. This is
the kingdom of the dead, abandoned by the sun,
where nothing blooms in the endless corridors,
and earth's sorrow presses down on us
like stone. Far above, in the weakened light of day,
under wheeling blackbirds, my mother waits
in the stubbled field, calling out my name.

Winter, Sleep, the Absence of Desire

After a long time in the darkness, the fur cloak
on her shoulders seemed like her own fur,
covering her skin with a fine, soft coat.
When her eyes adjusted to that place,
she realized it was not the solid black
she thought she'd fallen into, but an uneven
darkness of different shades and depths.
In her wanderings near the surface,
sometimes the light of day entered like an arrow,
and she could see outlines, edges of boulders,
streams, veins of quartz gleaming, crystals
in the granite shining out. At first,
she kept a lit torch with her always,
despite the long journey to the lake
of fire; now she knows her way
along the paths, as if she were surrounded by
another, larger body, but she has less and less desire
to roam, looking for a ladder to the world.

Instead, she lies curled in her mud-rimmed robes
in the small, smooth cave of dirt, half dozing, almost
content. In the silence she hears water dripping,
the slow breathing of the animals in their beds of mud
and straw. She wants only to sleep, to sink
into the dark, a mother who will hold and comfort her.

When she tries to remember her other life, circled
by blue, brightness falling like a shower
of flame, the images are small and dim,
like sunlight through the cracks of high
rock ceilings. And when she summons up
her other mother, waiting in the bronze
glow of autumn, her eyes are without pupils,
like a ruined statue; her once-strong legs are crumbling
beneath her; she is fading slowly,
like the memory of light.

In the Garden

Garden in Late Winter

Lost fragrance lost blossoms some cold green
eruptions jar lids and netting a few small
violas old upturned buckets and glass jars and wood chips
seed heads and snail trails leggy arugula dead vines
of green beans rotted nasturtiums rosemary blaring its little blue
bugles camomile sprouting and lettuces bolting
small brown birds searching nigella seeds bursting their
paper pods dead heads of sunflowers blackened
and flattened everywhere yellow-white fibers of
exploded artichokes still on the stem armored
like dragons sending their seed clusters out to the
wet dirt exposed roots and tubers oxalis springing
litter fermenting neglected and wizened weak
sunlight spilling over the Swiss chard and scaffolding
tilted my heart slowly opening like a dark bulb

At the End of the Drought

March gifts: All of a sudden, rain, falling every morning
when I wake, reassuring fine rain that will not hurt us.
And primroses, unabashed, cheerful as
crayons in the flower beds. Gulf streams of pollen
hazing the atmosphere; in Marin, wild irises growing
beside freshets and cascades, not far from where
the last few salmon struggle up streams broken through
to the sea by rain. My mother, born in March, who bled
from her poorly tied umbilical cord into the straw tick and lived,
even though her blood dripped onto the floor.
Inside, deep odors of jasmine and freesia; outside somewhere,
bees stumble, pollen-heavy, dazed
with what must be a kind of joy. So much newness;
even the banana slugs—bright, slow, cold—have come back.

In the Garden

She has it all, Persephone: roots and flowers, dark
and light; her mother, above ground,
baking bread; Pluto, in his shadowy hall,
dressed in black studded with jewels, like a rock star.
In the garden: nosegays of lettuces, cauliflowers like the tight
bouquets of brides; underground, bright carrot torches,
potatoes descending like divers in the darkness,
taproots of cabbages hanging, ghostly stalactites
in the fumey rooms.

Wet earth oozes into her sandals; she parts
fine root hairs, edges past tubers
and rhizomes, past sleeping chipmunks,
curled mice. The only light, faint sun through
gopher holes; the only sound, the animals' slowed breathing.
No days, not even time, just endless passageways
with sowbugs piled along the edges, earthworms
blundering through the walls, and Pluto's loamy chamber,
curtained with webs and lined with fur. All she has to do
is sleep, and love darkness, and surrender
to the night within her.

Until, again, as in a dream, the slumbering ants
and beetles start to stir; above them, soil grows warm
and crumbly as brown sugar. Beans curve their necks

like geese, holding aloft the white shell of the mother
between their simple leaves, and the stout
zucchini start their march across the garden bed.
Already, Demeter is waiting in the early light, cradling
a warm and yeasty loaf.

A Warm Summer in San Francisco

Although I watched and waited for it every day,
somehow I missed it, the moment when everything reached
the peak of ripeness. It wasn't at the solstice; that was only
the time of the longest light. It was sometime after that, when
the plants had absorbed all that sun, had taken it into themselves
for food and swelled to the height of fullness. It was in July,
in a dizzy blaze of heat and fog, when on some nights
it was too hot to sleep, and the restaurants set half their tables
on the sidewalks; outside the city, down the coast,
the Milky Way floated overhead, and shooting stars
fell from the sky over the ocean. One day the garden
was almost overwhelmed with fruition:
My sweet peas struggled out of the raised bed onto the mulch
of laurel leaves and bark and pods, their brilliantly colored
sunbonnets of rose and stippled pink, magenta and deep purple
pouring out a perfume that was almost oriental. Black-eyed Susans
stared from the flower borders, the orange cherry tomatoes
were sweet as candy, the corn fattened in its swaths of silk,
hummingbirds spiraled by in pairs, the bees gave up
and decided to live in the lavender. At the market,
surrounded by black plums and rosy plums and sugar prunes
and white-fleshed peaches and nectarines, perfumey melons
and mangos, purple figs in green plastic baskets,
clusters of tiny Champagne grapes and piles of red-black cherries
and apricots freckled and streaked with rose, I felt tears
come into my eyes, absurdly, because I knew

that summer had peaked and was already passing
away. I felt very close then to understanding
the mystery; it seemed to me that I almost knew
what it meant to be alive, as if my life had swelled
to some high moment of response, as if I could
reach out and touch the season, as if I were inside
its body, surrounded by sweet pulp and juice,
shimmering veins and ripened skin.

Community Garden

Why can't you want just this: sun and ocean wind
in the eucalyptus trees, old coastal pines,
a city built on hills?

Why can't you love your life, all of it, even
what you think of as your failures
and mistakes, just because it is your life;
why can't you give up the memory of pain and
your longing for the things you do not have?

Another of those bright, windy days
when I can't decide whether I have been blessed
or abandoned, the sharp edge of the continent
straining against the chill winds off the water,
the hard light of afternoon, and
I am trying to understand acceptance, to embrace
what is; down on my knees in the weeds
and the snail tracks, I turn
the sandy, neglected soil of my garden,
trying to love the imperfect world.

Rose Garden, Summer Solstice

Everyone here believes that the roses
are blooming only for them, here where the air
by the formal beds is layered with the scent
of roses. From deep in their flushed and darkening hearts
pour odors of lemons and pepper, apricots, honey,
vanilla and myrrh and musk and semen, apples and quince,
raspberries and wine and ocean, the faint
scent of blood and the fragrance of death and the breath
of the life we are living now, in this place
where the roses are blooming for each of us, alone.

To Dr. Williams

This is just to say
I never understood why
the plums were in

the icebox. Although
I like to think
of biting into chilled

plum pulp
before the shining door,
I keep my plums

on the kitchen table
in a bowl, where their dense
dark glossiness

grows as warm
as my own skin
and where

like small bombs
of ripeness
heavy with sun

and summer, slowly
their taut skin
slackens, splits,

and a thick, sweet
fermenting juice oozes
down each curving surface.

In Praise of Dirt

O, let us worship dirt, let us sing
in praise of humus and silt and leaf mold,
of worm castings and bacteria and minute particles
of rock, of all broken and rotten and stinking
things, for they are our home. Let us build a shrine
to the nematodes and the real toads
in real gardens, to the earth of enclosed safe places
and wild, free, dangerous ones; let us hold
the holy dirt up to our faces and breathe in
the smell of decay, the sweat and blood and excrement
of the Mother; let us mark our faces with streaks
of it like holy ashes; let us sprinkle it on our heads
like a blessing; let us lie down in it, sinking
into its cool grasp, and become part of it,
that sweet old place of time and history, bones
of our fathers, flesh of our mothers, everything
we are and what we will become.

The World as It Is

Unseen Eclipse

In my mind I see the moon—blotched,
rusted, radiant, shadowed, a ripe persimmon
growing sweeter in blackness
over the folded coastal range and its rough coat
of wild oats, snake grass, toyon, coyote bush—suspended
above the restless deer, the mountain lions
listening in the dark.

Haiku for Tassajara

*All things around us are asking
for our apprehension, working
for our enlightenment.*

—R. H. Blyth, *Haiku,* Vol. III

Driving too fast,
hurtling south through spring,
I poison the sky.

Green waves of hills
blued by lupine.
No houses yet.

On Carmel Valley Road,
counting toward
the 21.3 marker.

Unexpected snow
beside the road—
I burst out laughing.

Thick fog pours
over the far mountains.
Still more gifts.

Grader on the road,
this even more dangerous sea
of dirt and rocks.

After the hard winter,
we eat warm bread
beneath the trees.

Alone in my cabin.
How could it be
so cold?

Stream too high to cross.
The furry wisteria
begins unfolding.

Constant sound
of the stream.
Neither of us alone.

    In the steam house:
red- and green-streaked walls;
    air full of stars.

    Pouring hot
sulphur water on my head,
    I am home.

    No lights.
So close, the huge
    frightening stars.

    After firewatch,
I fall asleep,
    facing the wood-stove door.

    Narrow path.
Sheer mountainside.
    Cold fear.

Alone on the ridge.
A mountain lion leaps
　　in my mind.

Suzuki Roshi's grave:
black-purple iris,
　　lavender shooting stars.

Under the generous
maple tree, I lie down
　　on clean, dry leaves.

Driving home, I know
I will forget how beautiful
　　these mountains are.

Cachagua Valley, Mid-July

Clouds cover the new moon. Slowly rain
starts to fall on the dark mountains,
the crumpled hills. It reaches past
the hollow stalks of yellow grass
and is absorbed into the dust; it rolls
in streams off the shiny hooked leaves of
the live oaks.

The crows stir in their sleep. The horses
open, then close, their thick eyelids and sigh;
under the house, the old dog and the cats
blink and stretch. Inside, three women
half-awake, surprised by out-of-season rain;
miles away, forest fires begin to die
in the Los Padres.

Autumn at Muir Beach

Far below me, through the moving fog, the sea
boils dark turquoise and white. Suddenly
a deer explodes from his gray bed and bounces off,
his ears absurdly large, cinnamon colored.
The air is warm here on the headland, suffused
with sun and fog, the smell of dried grass
and chaparral. Something is expected of us:
some change, some awakening. The light
at a slant, the sun halfway down the sky,
every hour of the day touched with the sadness
of afternoon. Each moment palpable
as a berry, life and death joined at the core,
the flower against the bone.

Early October

So many bronze torches to lead us down
into darkness, dark lamb's blood
of dogwood, clear flames of sumac
and sassafras, and here and there, a few bright coins
for the hooded boatman on the shore.

Vermont, October

for Susan

Yes, the hills were on fire.
Yes, it was more than we could have
imagined, or could understand—
another reality in which we felt
overwhelmed, inadequate,
caught up in a wild celebration
we didn't know the rules for, stunned
by time racing over the hills, changing
everything as we watched, every leaf
dying its own particular death, as if
a beautiful death were the whole point
of living, as if coming to fullness, then
transformation, were everything, that
and color, drenched and radiant—
chrome yellow,
saffron, burnt
sienna, tangerine,
pomegranate,
flame, blood—as if all of life
were a green, steady
breathing, and death
an almost unbearably bright, ecstatic
letting go.

Crossing Mount Tam, Thanksgiving Week

November: The sun falls away
and the moon grows enormous, saying
I will guide you through
the pale nights by
this rising sea. Hills
the color of mourning doves,
the brown-gray of the deer
sleeping in their fragrant beds
among the dead wild fennel.
    The road rolls upward through
glowing, transmuted maple trees,
their big curled leaves
in bright drifts
in the damp folds of the ground.
So time turns gold and falls
away, and it's impossible to know
whether we are rising or
whether we are falling.
One by one the leaves
release their grasp to join
the layered place
of duff and mast and rot,
the faithful dark world
that will change us,
that will prepare us for
some new leafy crowns.

Finding the Petroglyphs

We walked down a road in New Mexico
past barking dogs, past gourds and chilies
on a fence, past the church and up
the dirt road to the water tower.
We hiked over the high-desert hills
of sage and chamisa and tumbleweed,
quartz and volcanic rock under our feet,
until we found them, scratched on rocks
the color of dried blood: a bull's-eye,
dancers, a sun-sighting labyrinth,
a turtle in a double ring, stick men
with testicles, and more than any other kind,
men on horses.

Below us the mother river opened the body
of the earth, releasing birds and fish
and willows. Around us were hills
patterned with piñon and juniper,
the trees dark yellow-green against the snow.
Over us the enormous sky of New Mexico
reached to the great hoop of the horizon.
I tried to memorize the landscape: dun-colored,
buff-colored, pyramidal, angular foothills
mottled with shadow,
gray-green winter-struck chaparral and

pale yellow bunchgrass rising to
escarpments and strata of rock,
colors of sand and pale-red clay,
broken layers and mounds and spills
of the unfolding of the land
in a country of lost people and lost words.
Now I am lifted over the Albuquerque airport,
high over brown suburbs and the thread
of the Rio Grande, miles above snow-dusted
mountains, a dry sea of *mal país*,
a vast mesa covered with waves of drifted snow.
I take out my pen and paper and start to write:
This is my spiral, my dancing figure,
my running horse.

Noche de Tumulto, San Miguel de Allende

The night of the storm in San Miguel,
we were sleeping in our posada close to the sky

on the altiplano, surrounded by cholla
cactuses and trembling mesquite and dozing

volcanoes, when the storm rode in and woke us
with its thunder, the rain rattling down

through the bougainvillea and rolling off
the pocked and striated stones of the sidewalks

of the pueblo, turning walls from the color
of mangos to the color of bull's blood,

washing the dust from the cobblestones
and the tile roofs and the rose-colored dome

of the *convento,* darkening the black-spotted
volcanic-rock walls and the crumbling

baroque facades of the *santuarios* and the pink
Gothic flames of La Parroquia,

and then it moved on over the fields,
drenching the black lava soil, and

the papayas and guavas hanging heavily
on the trees, and the flat roofs of houses,

their horns of rebar protected from lightning
by upside-down bottles, and it disappeared

over the sierra, and we fell back to sleep
in the house of the moon. But suddenly, the storm

returned, and this time it stayed for hours,
lightning charging the darkness like silver

on velvet, lighting the rooms just seconds
before the thunder broke and rolled on

almost forever, and then, filling
the spaces, bells began pealing wildly

in all the stone towers reaching
up to the clouds, and then, out of nowhere,

came the fireworks, fusillades bursting above us
in spirals and showers, and we remembered:

This was the feast of Corpus Christi,
the holy body, spirit incarnate

in stone and high desert and hot springs
and *masa*, and street dogs and old trucks

and calla lilies, and tropical birds
in the trees of the Jardín, and small fish

falling from the sky, and prickly pears
and rooftop flowerpots and wet walls

of indigo blue, so that when we heard
the brass band and the mariachis

pass by as the storm stopped and dawn
was arriving, no one was really surprised.

Landing at SFO

Then we began the long, slow mystery
of the descent, engines silenced, landing lights
spearing the dark, wing flaps louvering
like fins, the plane big-bellied,
awkward, tilting over intricate cities of light
lying below us like shattered jewels. Black
water, a necklaced bridge, bright diamonds of ships,
and us, angling down through black-purple stratus clouds
against a dark rose-umber sky. Quietly,
heavily, very slowly, like majesty, like priceless
cargo, we rode the night air down
until we landed, rocking, on the tarmac
and our lives started up again.

Driving with Robert

I was driving Robert downtown to pick up his new glasses. We were in my gray Honda with its rusted-out chassis and its one black Taiwanese bumper. We were talking about a book Robert was reading on particle physics and the expanding universe. It was after he'd stopped taking AZT, but before he got so sick he couldn't take the bus or walk more than a few blocks. "So, what do *you* believe?" he asked. "Well, I believe we're all part of one great consciousness," I said, amazed that someone had asked me. We were driving through the Western Addition, past barbecue joints and the Church of St. John Coltrane and filling stations and tall wooden houses with blistered paint. Robert looked at me as if I'd just given him a wonderful gift. "That's what I believe, too!" he said. "And I believe that that consciousness is evolving all the time." "That's what I believe, too!" I said. "And I believe that every creative thing we do, every poem we write or painting we paint or even every poem we read or painting we look at, somehow *adds* to that consciousness." "Me too!" said Robert. "And I think every good thing and every kind thing we do adds to it, too." His hair, which had always been luxuriantly thick, was now cropped close to his head, like that of a prisoner, or an initiate.

We drove down Haight Street, past pizza parlors and head shops and used clothing stores and corner liquor stores. The fine fallen dust of the universe lay over everything. The streets were full of people, each one part of the stream of longing. The city expanded and contracted like a great heart. "What do you think happens to us when we die?" Robert said. He was bone thin then, though still tall, of course. He didn't look like his old handsome self anymore, but he still had his full voice and his deep, rumbling laugh. "I think we become part of the consciousness in some way . . . but I'm not sure we keep any of our individual being," I said. "I don't know either," he said. I kept on driving. Outside the dirty car windows, the world rushed on. Nothing could stop it, or time's flooded river, or the fire all of us were burning in.

Night in San Francisco

Night clouds scumble overhead, some
racing through dark blue. The hidden moon
glides westward, steadily, while in the black
backyards, mockingbirds and mourning doves
and white-crowned sparrows and finches sleep,
not falling. Raccoons and rats shamble through
the trash doors, picking over cold pizza crusts,
stale French bread, rotten fruit. The morning glories
are pale pleated wads of lavender pink; night pools
in the throats of the trumpet flowers. In our small flats,
we sleep like bees packed in a hive. We dream that
our lives and bodies change, that anything can happen,
that we are just visiting, that everyone and everything
we've known comes back, that dark surrounds us,
that light returns, that we float above our bodies,
that we are not alone—and all the while, out on the edge
of land, the ocean rocks and shifts and folds.

Christmas Day

We have surrounded ourselves with things that perish:
candles, flowers, cut evergreens, children, friends.
The rooms hold more than we need of gifts,
of ornaments and sweets. And, all through the house,
the bitter perfume of the Christmas tree. After the feast
we linger at the table, darkness growing at the edges
of the room. In our glasses, bright globes
of carbon dioxide rise and break the surface of the wine;
outside the blind, wet windows, new leaves wait
deep inside the branches.

Tuesday, 9 a.m.

A cold morning, gray skies
and winter coming, and I'm running
down the sidewalk to my rusted Honda,
its faded paint job streaked
with rivulets of rain and urban grit,
in a quavery city of wooden houses
begrimed with pollution and astral dust
and scarred with human failure,
me with someplace to go
and not running late, my car
not yet leaking from the winter rains,
the Gipsy Kings on the tape deck and a poem
coming into my head, I think:
I love my life.

The World as It Is

No ladders, no descending angels, no voice
out of the whirlwind, no rending
of the veil, or chariot in the sky—only
water rising and falling in breathing springs
and seeping up through limestone, aquifers filling
and flowing over, russet stands of prairie grass
and dark pupils of black-eyed Susans. Only
the fixed and wandering stars: Orion rising sideways,
Jupiter traversing the southwest like a great firefly,
Venus trembling and faceted in the west—and the moon,
appearing suddenly over your shoulder, brimming
and ovoid, ripe with light, lifting slowly, deliberately,
wobbling slightly, while far below, the faithful sea
rises up and follows.

How Long Should You Look at the Earth's Face?

Until you have memorized it, feature for feature, so
you can remember it, like your mother's voice
in the room of your skull, speaking to you for the last time
over the phone, saying, "Are you happy?" Until
you are dumb with astonishment at having been given
so much: waterfalls, the ocean of air, insects
consumed with the world of insects, the sacrifice
of blossoms, fruit that ripens and dies.
Until you know that no matter what other life you live,
you will remember the smell of river water,
the chemical odor of ozone after rain, the solidity
of objects and the shadows that follow them,
food in your mouth, skin against your skin.

Notes

This book is dedicated to my friend Frank Prevetti.

The title of "How Long Should You Look at the Earth's Face?" is taken from a line by Rumi.

About the Author

CAROLYN MILLER is a writer, editor, and painter living in San Francisco. Her first standard collection of poetry, *After Cocteau,* was published by Sixteen Rivers Press in 2002. Two letter-press limited-edition books of poems, *This Is Mine* (2005) and *Constant Lover* (2001), have been published by Protean Press. Her poetry has received the James Boatwright Award for Poetry from *Shenandoah,* and the Rainmaker Award from *Zone 3.* She leads writing workshops in France and San Francisco.

*Sixteen Rivers Press is a shared-work, nonprofit poetry collective
dedicated to providing an alternate publishing avenue for
San Francisco Bay Area poets. Founded in 1999 by seven writers,
the press is named for the sixteen rivers
that flow into San Francisco Bay.*

SAN JOAQUIN • FRESNO • CHOWCHILLA • MERCED • TUOLUMNE
STANISLAUS • CALAVERAS • BEAR • MOKELUMNE • COSUMNES • AMERICAN
YUBA • FEATHER • SACRAMENTO • NAPA • PETALUMA

Design: Carolyn Miller
Text: Adobe Garamond Pro
Display: Futura Condensed Light, Didot
Printed on recycled paper by Hignell Book Printing